FULL

FOREGROUND

Camino del Sol
A Latina and Latino Literary Series

FULL
FOREGROUND

Roberto Tejada

THE UNIVERSITY OF
ARIZONA PRESS

TUCSON

www.uapress.arizona.edu

Library of Congress Cataloging-in-Publication Data
Tejada, Roberto.
 Full foreground / Roberto Tejada.
   p. cm. — (Camino del Sol: a Latina and Latino literary series)
 ISBN 978-0-8165-2133-3 (pbk. : acid-free paper)
 I. Title.
 PS3570.E435F85 2012
 811.54—dc23
                    2012013893

Publication of this book is made possible in part by the proceeds of a permanent endowment created with the assistance of a Challenge Grant from the National Endowment for the Humanities, a federal agency.

Manufactured in the United States of America on acid-free, archival-quality paper and processed chlorine free.

17   16   15   14   13   12   6   5   4   3   2   1

This is no place to be addicted to another place . . .
—*Exene Cervenka and John Doe,* Wild Gift

This is marvelous; it would be worth killing one's father for!
—*The "Rat Man"*

CONTENTS

ACKNOWLEDGMENTS

Grateful acknowledgment to publishers of the limited-edition chapbooks, literary journals, and anthologies in which some of these works first appeared: *Amulet Anatomy, The Broome Street Review, The Card Catalog Project, Conversations at a Wartime Café: A Decade of War, EOAGH: A Journal of the Arts, Gift & Verdict, O•blek: A Journal of Language Arts, Phatitudes, Rust Talks, Skanky Possum,* and *Sulfur.*

Very special thanks to Joel Bettridge for uncovering a shape in the dislocations; and to Tim Liu for points to the conclusion.

Prologue: The Archive Ballad

I am a concept after the natural end of two objects
I am the failed practice of self-rule a resource
Bent back more severely than the other moderns
Resonate or dog in minds away from their masters

I am in pornography a person not effaced
Or expressive of a single mood the arbiter
Of no one change brought about in relation
When mother to daughter is as pressure inside

The sorrowsong event or museum piece implausible
I am relevant to the material breech as weapons of
Destruction are to the symptoms of my tongue and throat
So united in a row as to stay the execution for a week

1. If Even Such Miracles Are Rare . . .

Piano wire of the last word said when it
once led to ginger-kissing any such son
invisible to himself, anfractuous. Mono-
logue for which there is no conclusion
no uproar no new guest amenities
no smile of the unforeseeable no nurse
to fill this rachitic prescription. Eroded
sources for public support, prosthetic
extension of the media, engineer to
employ me in this real and storied time
together as single and multiple
channels for the moving image
when this is written in the dark when
simulacra to surveillance as the secret
cause was to history in duplicate, original
demesne and mind-cure monument

IF EVEN SUCH MIRACLES ARE RARE

1

At the place come to a head by the assassins when images by way of
sound as in the beating below us, one floor down, maybe
two, her voice through some divide
neither one of us can locate, over
and over again her shrill
petition, and then a rumble
of a body thud, then still
and begging such that all
be rendered now of no account,
even less so the police,
the windows swung open to identify her whereabouts,
why now among the neighbors?

To this a mother's caterwaul between siblings
foaming at the mouth and panting with the punches
or so the predators, when to silence when
to speak as though an animal
were a benevolence and grace no longer
blurred between defiance
and threat, between money
and emotions, between
diplomacy and outburst,
between gift and verdict.

2

A year before the insurrection, I was terrified in my dream because
of all the resentful people, behind me, beside
me. They want me to get sick. The lower branches missing,
and every spark of the pines flared over the roadside
by the sun over the highland sierras
and down the valley outside Comitán.

That dream, the one of promised things, no work, no say,
no belonging, is just the envious people tormenting me. They want me to leave
          behind a weave of sickness.
They are angry since I built my little house.

3

Nocturnal nakedness in the clump field is
a clod of seedcake wrapped in oil paper,
furrows drizzled with mother's
milk, autumn kernels in gold riffle over
the earth to the last fistful of wheat
we called the bride as if to honor the dead
now wedded in a first blaze and middle surge
that brought us here, bread risen
from the pap of bone meal, humor
and the powdered grain grown
tall where our departed were lain
to face skyward in time so that
a downpour fell to soak the brittle
valley and the trees lending shade
beneath the ascending union
of our forebears, as we are here now
encircled drawing seed time
ground made wealthy earth
these harvest children wailing.

The intelligentsia of Los Angeles—a clover
leaf—is anathema to the Industry
composed of citizens so obsolete as to think
the elements of consensus and fit
are an act of translation or the willingness
to listen that allows for the true resolve
how many of us on line and in rank
when it all functions at lower best
Electronic velocity to deepen capital's
culture in the digital West an onslaught
by money demands and scientific compliance
in metropoles where rape is committed
every fifty-four minutes and the new moons
Caliban and Sycorax astronomers allege
by radiation dark-red into hydrocarbons
of old in the history of the solar system

As if still awake   daybreak   a brisk walk   *O moon my pin-up,*
chronometer   this inscription in heliotrope essentially chiseled
I suspect out of a rhythm transgressing now a soliloquy
whose logic lunches on the blood of lunation

and any keeper of Cybele's House no doubt may sup her
delicate fare bring the cup to lips and toast to you
comestible as whiting and ricecakes   bread and dates
and goatsmilk   to imitate an infant's mouth

around mother's tit to come all death-rattle over himself
and a belly so knotted as to parallel a speech more
than zero to himself or visible as a creature in language
in momentous kissing of an incubus whose

tongue down the throat inserted to simulate descent?
Charybdis now called Galofalo off the coast of Messina
by whose inertia any stasis in mother's discourse is
negated or by whose endless process is this becoming

of difference and absence so elongated the length of
the mind—waist-deep (giant steps) in snow—to surpass
certain limits even so: these cavities in which entire lives
exist of which I am utterly ignorant   (anyhow what's

left of that tenement on the corner of Attorney and Stanton
human head sinking as if whose last breath quicksand)

Animals   oblivious   stench of excrement
into the world armed with needles and
fangs at the moon in the forests of the new
England when savannas of Africa as
by any further reason for us to build a true
kingdom of God whose electorate's
advice on lawful matters concerning
witchcraft in courts of oyer and terminer
convene no longer
                    provided our brethren
abide suspected of collusion with
the accusers and their families joined in
prison by accident to spur memory.
Fornication by assault   salary   firewood

BLOOD
CHANCE
CHOICE

The kind of line I'm describing
when a tissue is severed

is to count heads when we were dying to
speak of what, as opposed to art,

between excess of image
or a towel to soak
                    the mess I made, this

udder-glove blemishing, the television
static in the perforated city

is a circle drawn around
the aftermath which is

a wax museum's prophylactic
limb   the deep-reader

diving into a cluster of life
forms and body parts

like barbed wire a witness
to half of what I should

have said. Red ribbon
by the demagogues,

this suspended breath
in place of nature

and love's lubricant
between the grip of death.

From examined blood
to minds that fail

when the gerunds
of becoming speak

the imperatives of
publicity. DELIGHT.

BE HUNGRY. LIVE ALL
THE ONES YOU WANT TO.

Being a day on which the eating of flesh
was forbidden, the monosyllabic, misdelivered
tug of the deprived body dancing
on the clumsy bone, earth
gleaming with blood of the unlawful,
the recurrence of first infliction,
or so the animal riven between my legs
in jets issued from the throat, gash
semblance of a human relish
in the agony of others,
as there were harrowed corpses
everywhere once here in uproar
and repetition over time
receding now into the ecstatic
lather and stench as you quiver
tight to the foul edge and fine gore

birdsong: insomnia

and the bulge of rubbish spewing from the mound
of bags left on a corner, does it matter where
or how meticulously sifted by the frail
scratch of a man there, anonymous atrocity,
this mere surface of miserable speech
at whose expense, what spasmodic drool,
whose squat life along the margins
of a public coherence bound only by malice
and raw with the hate of so much human
stink—as in the glower of the keeper
in surveillance never reconciled
between the executioner and victim

(Taxco: The Hills)

Limestone granite water
falls into foam of scrub oak
and lake line of the road

way cleft from the mountain
corrugated gush of bronze and
black the eye and ear straining to

render a motion of sight
and sound when there's none a
round   rubber tree   pine

palm   curvatures of earth
in mounded rise and blemish
green-gray suspense dulled

flax in a willingness to bear
the garland of immeasurable
weight   Antonym of hover

and smoothness   a fold
a surge   the sudden
drop a difference between

speck and encompassing stain
Distance between unattai
nable image and beholder

Source or matrix of a prior illusion
befitting the world now open to intimate
apex on the horizon made present in objects
rendered by mind over whereabouts   Frost-
bite a menace along the breakers I'm
craving this lavender black of sundown
in surfacing mounds of snow and when
we forego our soundness formal draped
or continuous as night figures along
Richmond Avenue or Ashland   How
might we get hard enough to follow orders
of smarter better-fit more masculine
the smell of animal feed   we who firefight
by rack and pinion   by mardi-gras bead

Newer measure to the ethics of a present
unseen or unsteady as a headlong drop to
the floor before government cameras
pulled away to the crowd in a televised
speech before the rally   A hundred thousand
of us in epileptic intent our flag to the forces
deployed in methods affronting vertical
threats no longer welcome to members
of student council no matter how far this goes
regardless of meetings we oppose until
begged by our teacher Mr. Miller on his knees
Signed, your friends who can't even with
laws in our favor a chorus of weapons
to skinheaded anthems androgynous

Field of material contentions and conflicts
in dreams of radical equality   market
by the name of liberal assets unleashing
in patterns uncontrolled so lawless
and brutal a concentration of wealth
and surplus such magnitude of deprivation
ever thriving to be more dissatisfied or
satisfied in a culture at odds internal devoid
of all patterns in civic life neither tolerant
democracy nor the promise of a unified
collective wager will survive its sway
as the final arbiter of the social good.
Prepared all told to safeguard the borders
of external threats to our security
lingua franca in which this is written
embody the moral bind   include us all

2. Full Foreground

FLATLANDS

The distinctive sign of nineteenth-century urbanism
was the boulevard, a medium for bringing explosive
material and human forces together; the hallmark of
twentieth-century urbanism has been the highway, a
means of putting them asunder.

—*Marshall Berman*

Given a body called the instant—and it's sprawling:

inside a prison house of vacant signs and overgrown environs
grim existence against the unimaginable
November light Memphis
rose of it brown behind sunset cloudforms
the rain occasional   edge
of the Mississippi River steel stretched green-gold
to an Arkansas sun fading into shifts of cityscape
flannel chills and on what side of the train tracks
where they now ban
the practice,
         the city having settled with relatives
of Adam Pollow, a University of Memphis student
who, four years prior, fell victim to a hog-tie
by officers of the peace—allegedly, else liable
—as he was belted with a night stick
shoved into the back of a squad car,
hands and legs now bound behind his back
a trussed animal rushed to the ward
where he's choking on vomit

                              or vacant signs
overgrown environs

               Temple in pentecostal elegance of dress walk worthy
of Enoch touching thousands through house-to-house prayer,
feeding the hungry, healing the wounded, clothing

the naked, building the kingdom, not only
the word but the enterprise of the saints
into the highways and hedges, highways
and hedges where I can rightly say
I have experience, making presence
known, which action of the Holy Ghost

idera

             espetani

                         rereson

and onto the empty lot of the drive-in along U.S.
61 on the outskirts of Memphis, sand-colored

pavement and the half-moons drawn by
speaker poles in rows concentric with desolation's

scribble of blackbird swarm behind the blank
screen   translucent dreary overcast

and lulled by the lapping of the wind and the onrush
of cars down the highway, thoughts of speed

and abandon, of pine trees holding back the bluff
and slope to honeyed voices from a picture show once

in desire and immanence: shall we gather at a grandeur
hushed by degradation and pointlessness

at odds with each other in the desolate stretches
of this smoldering kingdom devoid of

well, except for the low, poorly drained strip of land along the Gulf, the place rolling and fertile, the delta a broad flat region planted in soybeans and cotton from Woodall Mountain to the Gulf of Mexico, the point being where exactly in 1541 near Sunflower Landing

Hernando de Soto saw the Great River

HOUSE
TONGUE
TRACK

Three blind mice finger the alphabet song into ream is
my handle and spout by the culprits who, police
announced on Tuesday, were
chiefly married professionals
of whom you would have suspected nothing
but a sort of devotion

              Not unlike any other
relevant inquiry into the world, I mean the norm, not
the appearance, one of having been ransacked, about
a figure staggering among the arbitrary
pyramids of mango, tangerine, and medlar, around
the Chamula market, to the murmur of
children in church, the shuffle of feet
of knees over pine needles, but also
incense in rising seams, the shape of eggs
and bottles of Pepsi

              Something powerful
is lending lesser credence
to protracted visions fueled by a utopian
hope, the resentful people who want to do
me harm, or maybe the earth where the house was standing
dangerous, I don't know
what animal of well-being and destruction
led me to releasing bullets
between the eyes of the entire family,
propping the little ones up
against the bedroom wall
to watch me film myself all naked
over mother, real movie-like
to the camera, smashing every mirror
in the festering place to bury
shards into the corpses of mom and dad,

not that anything can be said,
or why this is a real person and the men
and women slaughtered in rural Mexico
are not compared to the public executions
of the official party's presidential
candidate or secretary general

                But is there room
enough for the pockets of my breathing
and the haptic glance with which I spread
the firmness of a lover's crevice against
my tongue, in consonants voiced
and unvoiced, hands dirty with the kind
of stroking that would sell you
a syringe, or the taste of money
I spend in the lube-city wet
dream, a share of compelling
stories to tell the master who
will reward me with license
over those in whose image
of a meaningful life I'd come
to play a prominent role

            when police said
they expect to make further arrests
with increasingly fewer means of establishing
the most elemental regions of thought
and feeling, any slogan impossible
—or so the television of ever escaping,
unequivocal and absolute, this
magnificent bondage

Not a word of my surrounding not a half-whispered
go to catch the rattled ought of a third concurrent

universe unlatched the more you wait, chalk drawn
thick of old around the marred bodies left

by the citizen squads our authorities facilitate, fail
to prosecute, guilt being therefore—quote/unquote

when physical comfort, when bodily prowess
and sovereign shape are rendered command

over the meaning of a nimbus once in sprigs
of goldenrod or Indian paintbrush, chalice

owing to rock crystal and featherwork, ivory!
carved in supple limbs, remote gazes and crusty

wounds, gold-leaf reredos in bellows pyramidal
from an organ pipe: an opulence wrought from

the nightmare of native oblation, of x-ian zeal
waged on local hands in effigies, Saint James

the Greater made in Goa and the Philippines,
or Rose of Lima, in a ministry of Indians

and slaves fallen victim to epidemic, heroically
to God and in penitential practice so extravagant

—cat claws and fish bones across her wasted
flesh—as to be the subject of ecclesiastic inquiry

into questions of faith, soundness of mind
stretched the length and breadth of his midrib

and torso in taut spasms, teeth clenched and lips
in a slather of animal darkness in time spent under

thickets, our twin intelligence a forearm and grip
in fast strokes around gleam and edge, tips

wet with each other, then deeper, to a clump
of hair and fingers guiding the back of his

head, mouth over gloss and curvature, blade
inextinguishable when too-slow a swelter released

in sounds of who, whose ah spread soaked along
his back and thighs rubbed sleek across

the wonder imperfections of form, lips abruptly
pursed to each moan pillowed by the sudden

hush of skin a spirograph, his dark upper
eyelids and lashes down his own limbs

now in aftermath-order and lucible enormity

Impulse in the great organism of terror whether with bombing
that led to throngs in flight from the sirens in light
   of global command

who at the helm on account of what strife means or survival
and so liable of the same murderous effect as

compared alone when I want this to deaden a kind
of blight in my head   sister the missing lips

of a mystified rhetoric or the paranoid moans about
cultural connections that do not exist   foresee-

able order of disclosure if a generation still reigned
in a state of sense and sound I object your

honor made plain and on what grounds have you any
right on behalf of the massacred when the last

word's a promise barely stomached between
equal-signs or the end-rhymes of a sonnet

describing the link between modern commerce and
empire   social category of race by means to

govern our colonial reaches with medicine and higher
learning   family and God overarching in ways

enjoyed as homeless tongues and twitches exacted
by teeth so close I'm all over my phobic throat

and chest around a windpipe in upper body panic
by a figure this Milosevic with war crimes

semblance of blame that of NATO's rejoinder
to the ethnic cleansing a life and purpose of its own

intellect severed from a body wrong in specimens of flesh
and branches under those I was ordered to

sleep all probe and tentacle a troubled fit when no
one visits in the interest of opacity or the last re-

sort a prayer that goes like this so listen   terminus
unburden our improvident fruit of all other riches;

umbrage, temper this stray unsobered will the cold
touch of the given   mother-of-pearl   levigate

our gash kinship—notch or hollow compelled
forever to my hispid thighs and maternal treble

DUMP
DITCH
KIND

Full foreground and shortcomings of this intercourse
if our voices mattered amid this kind of predictable
thinking, institution of secrets civil-silenced
or stammered-over without filling the gaps
in an ecstatic state

              of clashing
consonants when it all comes off the jack-end
behind the back-alley store-front in pull-back
sway I mean I couldn't care less
about anybody's private life, but it helps
explain why total incompetents, with no
knowledge of the language or society, are
running the show

              which is to beg it I
know and so self-inflicted I'm creaming over these
officers of the peace, joint chiefs of staff, no longer
anyone to punish me—and so extricate myself
from the weird undertow that kept me here to
begin with in acrimony of mind
and argument, in avulsion of what I weigh
when I tender you power of attorney . . .

As when a machine rises to the surface
of the present like the completion
of a past, and it's a point of rupture
from which a legacy will emerge
in the future, an evolution as per
all the creative forces of science art and social
promise, entangled in an emerging
sphere of abstract efflorescence, a blurring
effect over these agents of change
                in places

where local language is deemed
insurgent, these truant cascades
of speech repeatedly coerced into
dropping all that ornamental excess—of parse,
spell, and punctuate our thoughts
into the chilly spaces of the textbook if
we are to master the brawn
of power and knowledge,
a kind of opacity through
which the various will have
difficulty passing save in other ways
to be sorry I no say this more better
when the guh-guh-guys call me sugar or sweetheart

34

Caught between the last ground hideous and no
scratch for this hollow expenditure,
                                        I mean trapped
between the old art of the possible and this
global counterfeit for those
                                wrenched by
velocity penultimate, our well-intentioned trimming as
though patent with the shape of hands
                                        «where is invoked
the name of God, the Almighty will construct
a home for him in Paradise»

held to government notes across the carbon
stars of a dense winter sky pulled

out from under the chandler's wobble
of Earth
                        wrung down the purring
timbre of drop-bomb-seven whence blind
embossed hazard and boozy sentiment

are the repeated business of sense
and sound or money and prestige

                                transmission
speed of information now for those
who nourish their hatreds in the emptier
corners of the nation, who brood on

anniversary, as when how many members of Branch Davidian by
the FBI in the blaze and blister of Waco Texas (19 April 1993),
as when exactly two years after how many citizens and federal
agents in the death toll shards of massacre and bomb-fire-splinter
of the Alfred P. Murrah Federal Building in Oklahoma City, the
verdict now being McVeigh guilty on all counts of conspiracy, the
death sentence and

who gives so much as maybe the ubiquitous marvel of Heaven's
Gate styled sacrifice in self-expression and adult

urban content or meaningless loss as to presence,
personality, and purpose, against the

forced march to reduce our living standards, discard the old
resolves of equity
                              to lead "the process of
democracy in Mexico" or the tenuous
adhesion of events so immersed in

the delirium out of which way matters when
all this impairment this stammer is

exactly whose fallout and meltdown he wants to know

Low in tar and nicotine or menthol consensus
exactly a promise of mutual commitment

and also a process by time and a will this is
sending you signals severe as a surgeon

or generals who privilege this song if they
sing it unfree of embarrassment envy

and somewhere to go or a helicopter
ultra-lite in every polling station open or

supposed to be in 4 am lines the winter cold
stretched like approvals of how many miles

do we pledge an allegiance   Was it Alice
62 now voting in a township on the outskirts

of Pretoria and can I enter places barred
from me once if O is for office clerk

St. Louis April seven when harass-arrested
watchful as a body snatcher indemnify this

violation   Cuff me lieutenant to my new-
born in the back seat mister witness

my arrival and allegedly so we're suited
for each other over cars across the country

PRICK
PEEL
SHED

An establishment containing such a furnace stoked in
keeping with the authorities to show me these
projects are plausible, I mean short of marching
in pairs to provide a sense of homeland or nation
state—or else this must be some kind of a joke about
the confidence in a personality that will
coax you from disdain or
indifference, an altered voice into so much
sexual activity involving wet gels and latex, groove
or slot into which some part of an arrangement
of parts may suit my
identity to say of any assertion, it's
a failure, and a good thing I made so many mistakes
in the translation by dogs pulled to pieces, your
glasses full, our bodies cricking.

So be it. The matter pliable and less a question
of the contained, heretofore historical
place by which incidence will wither
whether hands testify to felt escape,
apparatus for us to be here who
make meaning a site of genuine
labor at the thought of blank
spaces of real stance indistinct
of any discernible shape and no
longer mine out of print as we
fashion a flawless ledger for us respected
citizens amid the throngs disabled by
misgiving, patriotic anthems into
lullabies, cradle song sleek
for the purveyors of wellness, homes
swelling with the complaint of victims
and counsels at law to say nothing of commerce,
first utterance or furtive decline, failed
weather anywhere and the classless strain

of entirely missing the point, drinks
nursed by friends in power, families
proud among the sinister ranks who
—because they draw parallels
between physical traits and the alleged
existence of an ethnic or racial group—
may well take the argument to its
logical conclusion and commit the same
barbaric crime as those bureaucrats
who during war and so forth in
such appalling excitement it
makes you shiver too close to the lower
last dilation of the firm drag in stroke
and wield along fold or fissure not
elusive to darting points of tongue
and orifice by deflect and contradiction.

It happens when the drift-rebounding of the wind's
a sound of flint to strike a spark from steel
understandings that were meant for us
here suddenly in the history of why
I have these matters to address, simply
things to say and a form to fashion a kind
of wholeness that begs no difference,
denies no fissure in the gemstone,
pries into the copse of it, says all
elements will move you forward in
time, the model more elusive
now than ever, if no one to fool.

As natural as hunger to a body,
a sheet of iron, a stalk of corn,
an agate in our hands claiming
the right to petition an assembly,
perform the seams of a nectar
drawn with bright nervous pulses
across the clearing of us here,
and the city there producing
lures to keep me penultimate
from the satisfied frets and roses
like warm milk. The haunted
matter hovering beyond reach,
teaching his lover to delay and
so it glistened like tourmaline,
a summer fruit in the moist air
as far as I was asked to crawl when
not entirely of independent means
to know the effort of body and mind
to an end, or useful for a special

purpose in sums payable in return
for services rendered by time in
wages per hour for the purchasing
of coal from India, gold from Brazil,
tea from Rwanda, and oil from Kuwait.

(Salgado)

3. Amulet Anatomy

Honeycomb perfection of this form before me.
No, not one imposing megalith, neither harrowing nor laughable
—the Coatlicue stone; or the monumental head of Juárez
by Siqueiros toward the ROUTE-90-TOLLBOTH to Puebla—
but the infinite combination of matter in myriad flux, each
  conduit
a machine in perpetual motion to generate the light
of all cities everywhere:
from this political navel to
the seamless outer fabric and the shadowhands behind
it, every interlocking part on the friezes at Mitla,
a remembered banter, a half-articulated sun
over what I'm getting at,

over these ruined phrases, see,
waking dull with repetition
and then I *vanishes with the dog-lights' sweet breathing*
over the cool wood of summer
and its countless diamonds spilling

"OK, so I sort of got the environs right as they were rendered
around me. Here now, they just hover in place," in/stead,
a chalk-choke foothold longed for,
rushing down Mexico City's metro, the smell
of burning rubber and baking sweat.

Wait. Not more than twenty miles from here,
in Itzamatitlán, an out-Lawrenced
repulsion—"inexplicable scent, in which
there are resin and perspiration
and sun-burned earth and urine
among other things"
—tossed into the dense air
in whose dry-wicker powder

of each page turned verso
from the 5-SUN codex
of what I need to know to make the work-day-week
ennobling, the whole thing
worth it and rage-
wrecked
or watermarked
by yet another PEMEX oil-slick catastrophe
off the coast of Coatzacoalcos when dictation
recedes of a sudden in ebb
and ejaculated glow

What it means to read Egyptian sailors voyage
to Byblos, the search for cedar wood in light
of manned exploration of space,
forthcoming places in which to raise the standard,
what I want from my enemies, the egg and bone,
the fingers burning when you get there.
But you fail in the process
at a velocity concomitant with the stuff and landscape
in front of you, overwhelmed by the lush pattern
around the slant horizon,
the distrust they claimed with regard
to language, the paradigm a spiral or side-long,
fretted angle always finite in a seemingly perpetual
clangorous tangle of immediate
meaning and whereabouts
on the tongue by which the acid bitter
sweet and savory
surround of the lace-sutured
writing and the force of the hand, or intrusions
like the telephone. This first wall
bears no fissure over the entry and habitual sameness
of address, not the violence
of home help me over the repeated
phrases of childhood
in slogans of television and radio
as per the language of Hollywood
and the roman catholic church
where time elapsed was a ray
beam the head now hovering
over thick air and feet
oblivious to the act of displacement
by which they may be said to exist.
Pull my arms then in opposite directions,
our lips wet now in the most

public of places, the isotonic pulse
and water lapped from flesh
to flesh, pulled
back to sway the thread
still joining mouth to skin,
then lifted from the fell
of it now taut, gasping,
inserted likewise, in arms, a slight
push to the next figure, legs
suspended and half-turned waist,
just the slight hairs
and slush full tongue over whose
agile hands and ass spread,
his shaft to navel,
tight grin a transparent
edge between laughter
and coming to the rip of too
much light when lips
at decisive points along
the exhausted places of repose.

A reverence in the order of time arises now some undersurface
into silk geometries of here therefore

                            observing this swerve
of lawful aim as pliant capacity curls
into what could be weeks of this unlikely touch

deserving tongue's synod plead the hereinafter
unto shores kept safe between the pages
of an ark outlive us

                        —escape and case in point—
render unshaven this day our cupped hands
unsure along the lilt of jaw rejoin

your collarbone   allure made
known and roseate and hollow
in the shape of lissome night
recede to surge again   my throat
moan in the fraught mind
and bodily intentions of is
this a kiss   a headswell grin of abandoned
contiguity of mouths
glide drunk with persuaded hearts'
surrendering apparel am I
watching these soft drawn
tenses of fragrant beige
or so inside your amulet anatomy

If there's no jeopardy to
these offices of the flesh
—jewel pressed against
this all-involving spot—
then it's a rapture uncertain
this company rare

and where on the horizon was it
over the summer so
numb therewith
now a winter hum
of knowing a science
something no
one need notice

if this is gift-given
or spellbound or
a thievery   else
this is dumb-struck
and falling asleep there
                              outside
of this rattle shall we gather
my vanguard of god
as we pleasure on
the other edge
of this election year
my luminary
in whose rogue
nation to imagine
a commonwealth
is to make impossible
any casualty
in this occurrence

Sun bursting as in water beads along his lower back and inner
thigh in awe derived from looking at a hero's naked body

aimless drift within made visible out of squint and second
sight or gleaming eager intake of breath a mouth full

stop short of lipped exhale elliptic against heft in mine
made immediate graze of finest hair   rise and pull

of his stomach, fist-grip and temples wet this heave of flesh-
hold in terms of reach and recoil   ample bearing hesitate

and limber shift enjoyed immersion glisten   from fore-
head and sideburn down the scar of his lower angle finite these

same words over and over what a face denotes in pleasured
reference itself a silver orbit tiny pierce at his nipple roused

thumb slick inside the hollow of my mouth   round
pressed with tongue and finger this is oil, liquid news, sway-

ed anticipation and too much reward the smell of butane
nothing hidden I'm outnumbered   every tongue in my ear

struggled sum of them in droplets distend   swell in me   this
is volume rippled mummery in advance of force poised

clutches deft in handle a weightless doubletake of a minute
the imprint my drenched face nestled in appetite and surfeit

I make mound of here his mouth a snarl an onrush ours a whole
surface impelled into fuck-yes abundance   glow-for-me

                                        Weather suited
not to a limitless field of occurrence, but to confinement,
an infinitesimal part of the alliterative outcome of how
and when to say it widespread, the entire keyboard,
palladian texture minded as in a piano music
listened to while nodding headlong off
into parallel motion with a change of position
during the alphabet years and a canon
at the lower fifth, hands crossing and thumbs
under in theme and inversion
to alternating thirds
                              with the aim of asking
what matter, what business to the tourist
whether the place is run by despots,
whether someone's been executed elsewhere
on the streets, whether the natives are
banned from beaches, or deprived of the water
used to fill how many swimming
pools, and why the climate is such
that we favor conditions where
moral values are established
in art and faithfully followed, like myself,
by sycophants in thatches of acrylic
plush in pink and black fabrics, feathery
torso and cunt in gloss or nipples
by leather straps petrified in the ideal
body a death wish. Or what happens
when you inhabit me thinking
here of each disordered instant with everybody
talking at once, all such a difficult web,
so many people to attend to, and not
regarding some arcane reference but the limited
world, all in the head, as it opens up to convince
you I am not formless, no matter

what the potential attempt
                              no matter once
in season when sound in dream
place delight and work of the vine
from furrows be praised the book of hours
whose clock-stop conceit over the house
of having unto higher ground I was
exhausted when I woke up
to the involuntary movements
and sensory impulse along the chain
of nerve cells, the collective
ashes and suspended
planks of the pleasure ward
wherein the human
shape surrounding certain
words was mint and glycerin,
drugs and explosives

VOICE
ACT
PLUMB

1

The plain terms this place a conversation where I reappear can hardly sleep
with sirens in the aviary amulets
to guard us, parvitude: where the failed
anchor of the everyday is a pale-green
egg-cup a paring knife a burnt match,
is a worm-eaten wooden box a quarter
pound of butter an alarm clock.
Alone now with these thirteen
words that will bring us back into being.
Watch where a purple script is
the jagged edge over which the drift
goes passing, as seen from the shoulder
of the highway not far from Oaxaca
where it borders with Puebla on the 125,
the smell of cowshit and brushfire
under the shadow of closing
thunderheads over the Mixteca,
off the road where we pull
and unbutton, your arms
in a Y to the sun, the dry heat of this
mechanical shine and motor
running in the dissonant
contours or rhythmic
five of what I like
about your body in bristle
and curl, the need to make
noise by feet in length
releases the kind of content
swelling when we touch
conclusive the ecstatic
cataclysm of the terrifying lull.

(Huajuapan • Iturbide)

The animal into parts—first slaughtered, in a body,
and then butchered, the blood-wet pelts
spread out to dry over trampled grass, the intestines hanging
from the chain-link fence
like the ribbed wings of a certain antediluvian something
is the matter with a newborn voice
bleating severance in which language
fucks me up in the smell of immolated flesh,
wet underbrush and mesquite. Slivers of it out to cure
from the day before are a stench
not a gravity in the air
as workaday and somewhere else
in the massacres we live with,
are a clove of garlic peeled, of Indians
by the Spaniards.

2

That she couldn't sleep at night without slashing her skin
as from the age of ten or twelve or else
the food she ate would razor steel,
would taste of being largely crosses on the surface
of an arm, a thigh, near a nipple,
into which the full weight
of her body now unleashed
was flying through the open slit

3

This nightlong rainfall is a hard zipper
when the cat's urine from the carpet
is about a house in no specific order, the cracked paint
on the ceiling an atrocity in the name of some collective self,
and the watermarks recalcitrant
to transformation,

ever changing,
                     a third of the text to paradise
when I one day write the horizon of the plural mind
unfolding in the rapid music rebound,
and I stutter, it's a pregnant shining,
cast against the walls now,
sufficiently warm, and a little juiced,
the joy of smoke through the nostril,
a final hit, a short unmediated dance
or gesture I would never make
in public, the ice-click in the glass
of lime and beer, the nearly midnight air
of June, and nothing severed
foremost. Someone coughing.

by what authority—as in the swollen
rhetoric of exactly whose enabling self

—am I next to you a gross paper
effigy when we wake to the sober

play of aimless bodies like and unlike
razor burn in drawl and daybreak

now near the south tower, or when
at the sound of this tone how a new

regimen of clipped tap and long
notes pressed against our wet embassy

trickled shoulder length in the tight
hush of what we know about

the difference between recessive
fade when pleasure sours

and the sore repetition of a song

Afterlife: Anniversary

Where on the morning, day in duplicate, was I without picture, to recall, day in sequence, holy ghost the telephone, ignoring the news, knows not, yes, that would be fitting, expedient, suitable, opportune, voice that begins with short hello, strong note, telling the item it stands for, speech trained to commit, ease tension, state fact, curtail information with such gladness as to eclipse a surname, disembodied, mine, it's the same

old ability to speak as ever, to this person for whom acquisitive I exist alone in the privilege of my household, as are these images on the television, and a voice skilled to submit in brief abridgment its business. An example is this— expandable for greater versatility, and with different features to match, in a portfolio free of risk, the key here, keep it compelling and to the point— *creeping horror* in real time of the unthink-

able impact arriving *in episodic bursts of chilling disbelief, signified first by trembling floors, sharp eruptions, cracked windows,* fireball through a building, *actual unfathomable realization of the gaping, flaming hole in the first of the tall towers, and then the same thing all over again in its twin* for a hell mouth, as civility to breaking point, fastened to this other voice in spirals listen closely

to what I say, for either it is yes, I am with you now, or no, the city disintegrating, revulsion somewhere, now everywhere, nowhere safe, and there in the picture is our talking, it cannot cease, it plummets also down the side of the south tower, in freefall, and a caller for whom *the merciless sight of bodies helplessly tumbling out, some of them in flames.* An example is this—it should have been enough for us,

to find me without recourse to oppose, but it wasn't, it wants me there, strapped between another transaction and catastrophe, like voice, for whose sake, I who am nothing, like it without cease. An example is this—say the kingdom in all its dust and debris, all the money guaranteed in cataclysm, on television, here together with me, our dividends in fourfold to enhance the hereinafter.

NOTES

Full Foreground composes a musical sequence whose desire is for lyric discourse to voice bodily sensation in the shadow of global command. It speaks of discontinuous times and locations on the borderlands of Mexico, the United States, and beyond, from 1997 to the present. The prologue poem was written in the weeks prior to the 2003 invasion of Iraq; the afterword, on the ten-year anniversary of the September 11 attacks, with language lifted from N. R. Kleinfield (*New York Times*, 12 September 2001, p. A1). From that duration and geography is reflected a language of current events, journalism, state demagoguery, the ethnographic account, and the pathologies of violence and massacre; extensions of a self—"myself"—in spaces of public address.

Flatlands: In 1997 I joined Mexican photographer Graciela Iturbide in her actions through the US American South, beginning in Memphis, Tennessee, south along the Mississippi Delta, then to the city of Opelousas, Louisiana, and its environs. I wrote: "Iturbide's vision turns an inverse anthropological eye to the emergency that can erupt from the most mundane phenomenon." The poem is indebted to the generosity of Rose Shoshana and Bruce Berman. In addition, another poem beginning "The plain terms this place a conversation . . ." refers to Iturbide's photographs of the *matanza* (or bloodshed), a commercial slaughter of goats in Mexico that has taken place each year since the colonial period, almost exclusively in the regions of Huajuapan de León (Oaxaca) and nearby Tehuacán (Puebla). More information on this photo exhibit is available online at http://www.getty.edu/art/exhibitions/iturbide/.

Dispersed throughout this book are a series of three-word clusters: concrete poems first imagined as television screen-grabs, later as campaign buttons appearing when "government cameras / pulled away to the crowd in a televised / speech before the rally   A hundred thousand / of us in epileptic intent our flag to the forces . . ." I worked in 2010 with artist Rob Verf who deployed the language to energize a nine-minute video: words, pasted onto Styrofoam orbs of various sizes, hover in an aquarium that gradually fills with water, forcing sphere and phrase into a gentle fury of movement and action. Today I submit the set as an intermittent totem of carbon thriving to matter.

ABOUT THE AUTHOR

Roberto Tejada is the author of two books of poetry, *Mirrors for Gold* and *Exposition Park*. An art historian, his other books include *National Camera: Photography and Mexico's Image Environment* and *A Ver: Celia Alvarez Muñoz*. He also founded and continues to co-edit the journal *Mandorla: New Writing from the Americas*. He is the Endowed Chair of Art History at SMU Meadows School of the Arts.

CPSIA information can be obtained at www.ICGtesting.com
Printed in the USA
LVOW080047160712

290180LV00005BA/4/P

9 780816 521333